WOULD YOU BELIEVE THIS TOO?

Here is another collection of supremely useless but totally fascinating facts. A book for the true connoisseur, this one, with a mind-boggling assortment of irrepressibly useless information:

The actor who played the part of Superman on television needed three men to help him out of his costume.

A young wife was granted a nullity decree in the London Divorce Court because her spouse was 'not a man'. The judge commented that there seemed to have been quite a serious deceit.

An American woman tourist hired a car to drive from London to Cornwall. She complained to an A.A. patrolman afterwards that the engine roared, lights kept flashing, she could not reach 50 m.p.h. and had used 54 gallons of petrol to cover 200 miles. The patrolman found she had driven the whole way in second gear.

Tarantulas can live for two and a half years without food.

**Also by the same authors
and available in Coronet Books**

Would you believe it?

Would You Believe This Too?

**Deidre Sanders
Dick Girling
Derek Davies
and Rick Sanders**

CORONET BOOKS
Hodder and Stoughton

Copyright © 1974 by Deidre Sanders,
Dick Girling, Derek Davies, Rick Sanders

First published by Talmy Franklin Limited, 1974

Coronet edition 1975

Designed by M. Mohan

Printed and bound in Great Britain for
Coronet Books,
Hodder and Stoughton,
St. Paul's House, Warwick Lane,
London, EC4P 4AH
by Hazell Watson & Viney Ltd,
Aylesbury, Bucks

ISBN 0 340 201452

There never was an age in which useless knowledge was more important than in our own.

Professor C. E. M. Joad

A TATTOOED man is more likely to go to jail than one without tattoos but is less likely to go to a mental hospital.

A NIGERIAN carpenter carved a model of Queen Victoria as a fertility goddess.

Two hundred thousand frowns make one wrinkle.

A 650 FT. salt mine below the Kansas prairies is used as a bomb- and quake-proof store for, among other things, 109,000 old MGM movies, the recipe for Wrigley's chewing gum, the city records of Chicago and Los Angeles, and the wedding dress of a lady from Wichita who is keeping it safe from moths until her daughter gets married.

THERE are seven million lamp-posts in Britain.

ANGELO Faticoni, the Human Cork, once swam from Manhattan to Hoboken tied in a chair weighted with 40 lb. of lead.

A HUMPBACK whale can eat 5000 fish at a single sitting.

POPULAR items on sale in a Harlem magic shop included Follow-me-girls Powder, price 1.50 dollars ("Sprinkle it on your shoes and become irresistible to women"), and Get Rid Powder for 2 dollars ("Sprinkle it on your door sill and rent, bill and instalment collectors will pass you by"). Also on sale were Death Prayer Candles and Vanishing Powder—much prized by criminals wishing to cover their tracks.

SIR David Ochterlony, British Resident in Delhi, had 13 wives.

AN Australian student was arrested on a charge of offensive behaviour for walking down the street dressed as a sealion.

Beware all stage-door Jacques at the Crazy Horse Saloon, a Parisian strip-club; the owner of the club engaged the entire French national judo team to teach his girls self-defence.

A NINE-YEAR-OLD visitor to South Shields Museum, Co. Durham, correctly identified a "Roman sesterce coin from between 135 and 138 A.D." as a plastic token given away by a soft drink company.

IN the 10th-century Japanese court, the way you handled a brush was considered to be better indication of your character than what you said or wrote.

THOUGH 1 mg. of fluoracetic acid will kill a dog, toads have been known to survive a dose of 10,000 mg. without turning a wart.

A Frenchman murdered two wives because he didn't like their cooking.

AMONG the costumes sported at a New York fancy-dress ball thrown by film director Federico Fellini were 227 cardinals, 143 nuns, 95 Southern belles, 63 S.S. officers, 21 birds of paradise and four Adolf Hitlers.

Young men think about sex once every 15 minutes.

THE most effective method of cleaning your teeth is to chew on a stick; second best is using a towel on your finger; third is toothpaste and brush.

A LETTER posted in New York arrived in Ohio three months later having travelled by way of Canton.

MORE than half the men of Corfu are called Spiro.

Marie Antoinette and Jayne Mansfield had identical bust measurements.

THE Nigerian miracle fruit is tasteless when eaten on its own but has the power to change the taste of other things. Thus a lemon eaten after miracle fruit can be mistaken for a sweet orange.

Two totally blind football teams played a 2-2 draw in Lima, Peru, using a sonic ball containing a handful of dried peas.

*Rats are extra-vulnerable
to poison because they are
unable to vomit.*

INNER London's bird population is between 23,000 and 45,000 pairs, mainly sparrows and pigeons.

HENRY I decreed that the yard should be the distance from his nose to his outstretched thumb.

A PAIR of sparrows make some 5000 hunting trips during the three-week period before their chicks leave the nest.

WHEN Princess Anne married Captain Mark Phillips, on November 14, 1973, Royal Mark won the 2.30 Wedding Stakes at Wolverhampton.

A LETTER posted in Bromley, Kent, arrived 37 years later at Thorogood, Sutton-at-Hone, 12 miles away. The Post Office demanded 6p excess postage.

THE first edition of *Infant Care*, published by the U.S. Government in 1914, recommended the use of peat moss for disposable nappies.

THE Greek Parthenon has been damaged more severely by pollution during the past 25 years than by any other cause in the previous 2000.

LAOTIANS measure distance in terms of the time it takes to cook rice.

A 400-YEAR-OLD English traditional song was banned from American television because it contained the word 'maidenhead'.

If the British national debt were stacked in £1 notes the pile would exceed 2500 miles.

A ZOO gorilla was cured of constipation by being shown the head of a turtle, which he mistook for a snake.

CHINESE babies' births are celebrated after 30 days, after one year, and then only at 10-year intervals.

THE spirit distilled from a quart of beer was given to two dogs at a temperance rally in North Meols, Lancashire. One died on the spot, the other a day later. Several drunks promptly signed the pledge.

A LOS ANGELES school board tried to ban Tarzan books because the hero lived with Jane in a tree house *and they weren't married*.

ELIZABETH I kept 80 wigs.

Each inch-long Colombian tree frog contains enough venom for 50 lethal poisoned arrows.

THE Frenchman St Evremond, a favourite of Charles II who drank nothing but champagne, was appointed Governor of Ducks' Island, at a salary of £300 a year. The island was constructed as a refuge for waterfowl in the lake in St James's Park.

An American nuclear scientist, Theodore Taylor, claims that any reasonably intelligent person could build his own nuclear bomb from ingredients which are, mostly, easily available.

PERHAPS I COULD START BY GROWING A BEARD...

'Kami', the Japanese word for god, is an abbreviation of 'kagami', meaning mirror. In Shinto thought, a mirror is a symbol of god.

THE taste-buds of the tortoise are 40 times less sensitive than those of mammals to certain poisonous alkaloids in plants.

HOMING pigeons can exceed 90 m.p.h.

A SERIES of baffling fires in an Ohio rubber factory was finally traced to a young woman whose body was found to carry an electrostatic charge of 30,000 volts. Her resistance was 50,000 ohms.

Air hostesses have the lowest divorce rate among working women.

IN the mid-19th century, London's smokers discarded 30,000 cigar butts every day.

The Chinese in Borneo use pythons rather than cats to keep down the mice in their boats and houses.

A MAN brought before Teesside Crown Court in May 1973 for showing contempt by raising two fingers at a car bearing a pair of High Court Judges was released when the court heard his explanation. He thought it was the mayor.

Fear of impurity prevented nuns removing their clothes to wash until a hygienic vision revealed to St Brigitte that the Lord would have no serious objection to a proper hot bath once a fortnight.

Argentinian gauchos sometimes lay slices of raw beef underneath their saddles; after a hard day's ride the meat is tenderised by the rider's seat and cooked by the heat.

IN 1970 the average Briton consumed $3\frac{1}{2}$ lb. of coffee and $8\frac{1}{2}$ lb. of tea. In the same year the Swedes drank their way through $28\frac{1}{2}$ lb. of coffee each.

MR Fred Palm of Lansing, Michigan, was awarded life imprisonment for being caught with a pint of gin during Prohibition.

EVERY time you take a step forward you use 54 muscles.

THE meat from an average rabbit contains the nutritive value of $4\frac{1}{2}$ lb. of beef.

MRS PUCCINI, wife of the Italian composer, steeped her husband's trousers in camphor and put bromide in his coffee when attractive women came to dinner.

ASA SOULE, an American patent-medicine mogul, offered 100,000 dollars to the University of Rochester to change its name to Hop Bitters University.

ABOUT half-a-million Britons take snuff.

IF two people agree to commit suicide together and only one is successful, the survivor is guilty of murder under English law.

THE world's only wild camel herds are in Australia.

Between 1589 and 1607 at least 4000 French noblemen were killed in duels.

A POLAR bear can reach a speed of 25 mph on ice.

AT Cedar Lake, Indiana, a 100 lb. watchdog looked on impassively while two men raided his master's business premises. Then he bit the policeman called in to investigate.

LONDON'S highest rates of suicide are found in Chelsea, Holborn and Hampstead.

A TWO-YEAR-OLD sheepdog in the East German village of Wilmersdorf grew a spare set of ears.

THE annual budget of the United Nations Food and Agricultural Organisation is less than the expenditure on snow-clearing in New York City.

A notice outside an Amsterdam strip club promises: "No erection—money back."

A POPULAR hair-style in England at the time of the French Revolution was known as "la coiffure à la victime", in which the hair was cut short and dishevelled, and a crimson ribbon was worn around the neck.

A SHOP sign in Streatham, south London, reads: "Funerals, wreaths and bouquets. Potatoes a speciality."

OF the world's 360 known species of oak, 130 grow in Mexico.

Saturday, Sunday and Monday are the wettest days in the English week.

A WOMAN in Herne Hill, London, woke up one morning to find the dead body of a man wedged in her bedroom window. Police deduced that he was a burglar who had died from a heart attack.

A Brazilian state governor once appointed 600 persons to the official post of State Taxidermist. He collected the salaries of all, and also pocketed the state's highway budget of nearly six-and-a-half million dollars.

A male bower bird needs to be endowed with considerable artistic flair if he wants to cut a dash with the ladies; he must decorate his bower with shells, berries, leaves and flowers. Even though mating takes place inside his masterpiece, the couple later move out into a simple nest up a nearby tree.

SNAILS can sleep for three or four years at a stretch.

THE sale of patent medicines—such as Kennedy's Medical Discovery, Kickapoo Indian Sagwa and Hamlin's Wizard Oil—had reached 80 million dollars a year before the U.S. Government started cracking down on them in 1907.

IN 1963, an American Government manual advised doctors screening immigrants that a Pole could be considered exceptionally bright if he could recite the months of the year in reverse order.

THE Chinese newspaper *Shantung Peninsula* reported that 14 women were ordered to breastfeed a litter of 14 piglets because the sow's milk was sour.

*A Suffolk dairy collected 1800 empty milk bottles
from the home of a single elderly woman.*

The Emperor Maximilian ordered the two rivals for his daughter's hand to fight a duel, the winner being the one to place the other inside a large bag.

SPREAD out, the walls of your intestines would cover 100 sq. ft.— five times the area of your skin.

England consumes one-third of the world's boiled sweets.

IN the 18th century an African King of Karagwe liked his wives so fat that they could not stand upright and could only grovel on the floor like seals. Their only food was milk which they sucked, without interruption, through a straw from a gourd. Young girls who resisted were force-fed.

AFTER 84 days in space, the three astronauts on America's last Skylab mission had each grown 2 in. taller.

KANGAROOS are 1 in. long at birth and grow to 8 ft.

BETWEEN 1940 and 1945 the rabbit made up 10 per cent of Britain's meat ration.

UNTIL 1879 soldiers in the British Army guilty of bad conduct were tattooed with the initials B.C.

AN adult breathes about 7,844,000 pints of air a year.

You can eat your way to a criminal record. A survey of 3000 juvenile offenders showed that most of them had been living on a diet of cake, chocolate, biscuits, ice-lollies, white bread and Coca-cola. This led to a deficiency of vitamins B1 and B12 which, researchers said, can lead to schizophrenia and anti-social behaviour.

GIVE US A BREAK, YER HONOUR — HONEST, I WAS CAKED OUT OF MY MIND

To prevent their being separated by their watery couch, families of sea otters bind themselves together with strands of seaweed before going to sleep.

ONE acre of English field is home to two-and-a-half million spiders. The length of web they spin in a day would stretch round the world; in 10 days it would reach the moon.

The average American car is idle for 22 hours a day.

THE armistice ending the First World War was signed on the 11th hour of the 11th day of the 11th month of 1918.

MARIJUANA was prescribed by Chinese physicians as a remedy for gout, rheumatism, malaria, beri-beri and absent-mindedness.

New York City boasts a kosher Chinese restaurant.

MOTORISTS without the 50 cents toll needed to cross San Francisco's Golden Gate Bridge are allowed to leave collateral. An auction of deposited items included various shoes, tools and tapes of rock music, four cans of lima beans and five men's wedding rings.

You are more likely to die from a lightning-strike in England than from the bite of an adder. Snakes killed only seven people between 1899 and 1945.

IT is unlikely that Cleopatra actually committed suicide with an asp, as the species is unknown in Egypt.

No new building has been put up in Dubrovnik since the 18th century.

THE Malay equivalent of "to take a walk" is, literally, "to eat the wind".

A British firm markets underground fallout shelters for pets.

A 16TH-CENTURY Dutch map shows Scotland as an island with York one of its major cities.

A GRIMSBY firm specialising in weed-free turf for sports pitches decided to add to their range grass-free weed in the interests of ecology. This 'nature conservation blend' was intended to restore to the countryside "many of the delightful weeds that are so necessary to wildlife". A 30 lb. pack of weed-seed cost £1.50.

A snail, one of nature's most fervent lovers, is equipped with both male and female reproductive organs on its head.

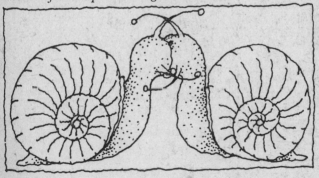

IN 1843 two French gentlemen, Lenfant and Mellant, quarrelled over a game of billiards and drew lots to see who should first throw the red ball at the other. Mellant won and hurled the red accurately at Lenfant's forehead, killing him instantly.

IN the Somali language a satellite is "a star that failed to reach Heaven".

THE world's tallest hedge is in Scotland—at Meikleour, Perthshire. It is 85 ft. high, 600 yards long and was planted in 1746.

JAPANESE building workers used to employ kites to carry bricks to the top of tall buildings.

ORGANISERS of the World Gliding Championships at Waikerie, Australia, advised competitors to beware of wedge-tailed eagles. Defending their territory against such well endowed rivals, the birds attack pilots to an altitude of 10,000 ft.

Flowers for Queen Victoria's funeral cost £80,000.

To help promote birth control in India, the three wise monkeys were blessed with a brother. Brass-monkey sets on sale in the shops included not only Messrs. See, Hear and Speak-no-Evil, but also Do-no-Evil, clutching himself with appropriate coyness.

TANKS ordered out by the Government to control the turmoil in Rio following the suicide of President Vargas were considerably delayed by traffic jams. When they finally reached the presidential palace, tanks from an opposing faction in the army had already arrived. The enemy crews proceeded to play a game of football, using the tanks as goals.

Guadua trinii, the Argentinian cane plant, has the world's most advanced biological clock. It produces seeds exactly 30 years after its own seedhood.

IN 1809 the Rev William Cowherd made total abstinence a condition for membership of his Bible Christian Church of Salford. After completing a vast tome of 6144 numbered articles illustrating Bible truths, Cowherd died of a disease induced by over-studying and lack of physical exercise.

Until 1940, fish-frying was officially classified as an offensive trade. But from October 1 of that year, chippies were no longer categorised with blood-boilers and gut-scrapers.

A 30-YEAR-OLD taxi-driver in Christchurch, New Zealand, was awarded £10,310 damages after he went into hospital for an operation on his hand and was sterilised by mistake.

MR Lancashire is president of the Blackpool branch of the Yorkshire Association.

LONELY cats and dogs in the United States can meet each other through marriage bureaux.

The Christian names of the first couple to be married in the parish of Greenock, Scotland, were Adam and Eve.

THE greengage was introduced into England in 1725 by Sir William Gage.

To pierce the boredom of a particularly gruelling reception, President Truman muttered to everyone he met: "I murdered my grandmother this morning." Nobody blinked—except one man who growled back: "She had it coming to her."

GEORGE II took such an interest in his food that he ordered every dish served to him to be labelled with the name of the chef who had made it.

A GROUP of schoolboys nominated a leading dermatologist as the "sportsman of the year" because he wrote that "skin diseases in civilised countries due to excessive washing are commoner than those attributed to dirt".

LYNDA Bird, daughter of Lyndon Johnson, wore earrings made of two tiny cages, each containing a live bird.

A TYPICAL Victorian Royal breakfast consisted of five courses. There would be an egg dish, bacon, grilled trout or turbot, a meat dish, and woodcock, snipe or chicken. But the Queen herself ate only a boiled egg—scooped with a gold spoon from a gold egg-cup.

After the death and discredit of Beria, chief of the secret police, Russians were told to tear out references to him in their encyclopaedias and replace them with an entry about the Bering Sea.

WHEN threatened, hognosed snakes of North and Central America roll on their backs and feign death. When turned the right way up, they give the game away by instantly reverting to their "dead" posture.

AN advertisement in the personal columns of the London *Evening News* invited young ladies seeking adventure to meet a well set-up gentleman with honourable intentions. When four or five thousand women turned up at the rendezvous at Piccadilly Circus, police had to be called in to control the crowds.

IF the world were 50 cm. in diameter, the crust would be the same thickness as the skin of a balloon of the same size.

AN ALBATROSS can glide for up to six days without beating its wings, taking the occasional nap while airborne.

A blonde Venezuelan stripper who performs nightly at a club in Caracas writes to her mother every week enclosing a doctor's certificate to show she is still a virgin.

The first alarm clock, which woke the sleeper by gently rubbing his feet, was invented by Leonardo da Vinci.

RUSSIAN scientists found a live lizard in a chunk of Siberian ice 33 ft. below ground level.

THE rudder of a giant oil tanker is large enough to park 47 small cars; the deck area is equivalent to two football fields or 79 tennis courts; and the height of the vessel is equal to a 23-storey sky-scraper.

A JAPANESE civil pilot who landed by mistake at a Tokyo military base explained his error: "I was confused by the rays of the setting sun."

Unlike most fishes, whales can't swim backwards.

ST Germans Rural District Council, in Cornwall, voted by an overwhelming majority in favour of film censorship. The district has no cinema.

THE air fare for a Briton emigrating to New Zealand early in 1974 was £262 for himself; £320 for his Alsatian dog.

EVERY day, America swallows the contents of more than 70 million cans and jars, and upwards of 32 million lb. of frozen food.

THE Securities and Exchange Commission, a Government agency which supervises America's stock exchanges, filed a lawsuit early in 1974 to prevent a consortium of German businessmen selling American investors shares in a brothel. Their complaint was that the Germans had failed to justify their claim that shareholders would double their money within 10 months.

During Columbus's fourth voyage, his crew waited until nightfall before tucking into their meal of crumbled-biscuit porridge, so that they wouldn't see the worms.

When a goalkeeper disputed a goal during an amateur football match in Mexico City, the opposing centre-forward ran to the dressing-room, returned with a pistol and riddled him with bullets.

IF you weigh yourself immediately before a meal and then four hours afterwards, you will often find you are lighter as a result of moisture-loss through skin and lungs during the process of digestion.

CLEANER wrasse, which live in the depths around the Great Barrier Reef, live in groups of about a dozen female fish dominated by one male. If the male is removed from the group, the largest female assumes his role and undergoes a spontaneous sex-change.

Americans consume on average 60 gallons of water each day.

THE TALLEST MP elected to serve in the British Parliament in February 1974 was 6 ft. 6 in. Spencer Le Marchant. He was returned by High Peak, Derbyshire.

The upkeep of the Royal Family costs each Briton 2p a year.

AT one stage in the early development of New York, one house in four sold alcohol.

THE Prime Minister ranks 11th in Britain's Order of Precedence.

TRAVELLING at its prime cruising speed of 2 in. per minute, an athletic snail could complete the Olympic marathon in 550 days.

A Swedish doctor weighed patients before and after death and calculated that a human soul weighs 21 g.

ONCE he had taken to wearing wigs, Louis XIV would permit only his hairdresser to see him without one. When he went to bed he insisted on passing his wig out to a page from behind the drawn curtains of his four-poster, reversing the process in the morning.

PRISONERS in an Ulster jail complained when their subscription to a magazine called *How It Works* was banned. The first issue had contained detailed instructions for making atom bombs; others had explained automatic pistols, armour-piercing shells and anti-aircraft guns.

A BRITISH dentist left nearly £200,000 to his nurse, on condition that she did not wear make-up or go out with men for five years after his death.

IN 1800 the poet Coleridge was taking over half a gallon of laudanum, a solution of opium, every week.

SPINSTERHOOD is unknown to the Tiwi women of the South Pacific. They are betrothed to adult males while still in the womb and married at birth.

Rape is not an exclusively human activity. Birds do it too.

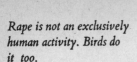

FOURTEENTH-CENTURY butchers found guilty of selling bad meat were put in the pillory and had the meat burned beneath them.

DURING the Middle Ages, pigeons were the chief source of fresh meat in Britain.

AMONG the words forbidden for many years by Hollywood's self-imposed code of decency were 'cocotte', 'courtesan', 'madame', 'wench', and 'sex'. The code also stipulated that "the expression 'travelling salesman' must not be used where reference is made to a farmer's daughter".

A snail can have up to 25,600 teeth.

WHEN a bar in California offered "all the beer you can drink for a dollar", a Mr Glenn Moore took up the challenge. He swallowed 16 pints in four hours and died.

Dolphins used in striptease shows have their task of removing the young ladies' bikinis made more appetising by the garments being soaked in liquidised fish-meal. The girls are trained by a toothless frogman.

A 15-YEAR-OLD Sydney boy failed to persuade Qantas to pay him half-a-million Australian dollars in return for not destroying one of their airliners.

SIXTY years after the outbreak of the First World War, Germany agreed to compensate Greece for merchant shipping sunk by the Imperial German Navy.

PAINTER Ad Reinhardt's most valuable work, a plain black canvas 5 ft. square, fetched £24,000 at Sotheby's in 1974.

THE smoke produced in Britain in one year weighs between two and three million tons.

A VAN-BOY in Maryport, Cumberland, was fined £10 after he had thrown a Mars Bar out of his van window and knocked a professional wrestler unconscious.

Each Briton consumes an average of 273 eggs a year.

THE American cicada mates only once in his 17-year life, and dies immediately afterwards.

At a Manhattan restaurant called Group Therapy, psychologists conduct collective analysis sessions over meals.

For American whites the suicide rate is five times as high as the homicide rate. The reverse is true for blacks.

IN 1852 the London Necropolis Company opened a vast cemetery at Brookwood, near Woking, Surrey. It had a private railway station adjoining Waterloo, its own trains, two stations in the cemetery itself, with the nameboard Necropolis, and the telegraphic address of Tenebratio, London.

MORE Americans were murdered in the U.S. between 1970 and 1972 than were killed in 10 years of the Vietnam War. The murder rate is 48 times higher than those of Britain, West Germany and Japan combined.

A LONDON clergyman who was knocked down by a lorry was awarded £8000 damages because he could no longer kneel to pray.

ONE of the first results of the Eskimos' contact with whites (when Peary, first man to reach the North Pole, set up a colony) was the Floradora Sextet, an amateur can-can line of Eskimo girls.

THE most popular music among patients at the artificial limb centre at Roehampton is Sousa marches.

A LARGE blue whale needs three tons of food every day.

Two women in Louisville, Kentucky, inherited an estate worth 115,000 dollars from their late aunt's goat.

THE Japanese believe that disaster will surely follow if *kiri* leaves fall to the ground too early. During the Second World War the American Air Force tried to induce panic by dropping thousands of leaf-shaped pieces of paper.

PRISONERS on the treadmills at Warwick Jail used to climb a daily equivalent of 17,000 ft.

A JUNIOR accountant, Mr Ahmed Corker, was passing through customs at Manley Airport, Jamaica, when a large rat dashed up and sank its teeth into the sole of his shoe. After the rat had been repulsed, customs officers discovered that both of Mr Corker's shoes were soled with cannabis.

WHEN sea-bathing first gained popularity, 'dippers' were employed to hold wealthy clients against the waves and ensure a thorough soaking.

THE sun contributes 99.87 per cent of the solar system's weight.

It costs the State more to keep a boy at an approved school than it would to send him to Eton.

...SO DOMINIC AND I DECIDED TO PUT HIM DOWN FOR STRANGEWAYS

Cookery books outsell sex books in the United States by three to one.

Giraffes are particularly susceptible to throat infections because they can't cough.

IT costs up to £20 to have your plant's illness diagnosed at a plant hospital in the United States.

PENGUINS can gather enough speed underwater to leap 7 ft. or more into the air.

IN 1824 two practical jokers named Lozier and De Voe succeeded in convincing many New Yorkers that the southern tip of Manhattan was about to break off because it was too heavy. When they proposed that it should be sawn across and put the other way round, a crowd of 500 people and 50 hogs met at the Bowery to march with fife and drum to the sawing-point.

A LEADING cabaret attraction in San Francisco is "a topless grand-mother of eight".

PLACE-SETTINGS at Buckingham Palace banquets are measured with a ruler.

A FULLY-LADEN Concorde and a single-occupant family car both do 30 passenger miles for each gallon of fuel. The most extravagant user of fuel is the QE2 which, with a full passenger-list, can manage only 12 passenger miles per gallon. Most economical is a 12-coach diesel train, giving 642 passenger miles per gallon.

There are 150 million bicycles.

WE EAT up to 70 tons of food during an average lifetime.

THE electric blanket was invented in 1949.

THERE is enough water in the world's lakes and rivers to flood England to a depth of one mile.

A NORWICH delicatessen arranged for a mercy flight of Aberdeen haggis during a rail work-to-rule for the benefit of expatriate Scots who feared they would be unable to celebrate the 1974 Burns night in the traditional way.

THE only country to issue stamps commemorating the International Free Balloon Races was Poland, which overprinted two existing stamps with the legend "GORDON BENNETT 30.VIII.1936" in honour of the founder of the races.

IN Ancient Greece, senior citizens on the island of Kea were expected to drink deadly hemlock on their 60th birthday.

MICHAEL Todd Jr. took advantage of the Smell-o-Vision process to make his film *The Scent of Mystery:* 52 different smells were blown at the audience at appropriate moments in the action.

A CHINESE businessman in Hong Kong paid £2800 for the car registration 8888. In China the number eight is supposed to bring prosperity.

MORE bicycles than cars were sold in the USA in 1973.

A MODERN jetliner consumes 35 tons of oxygen on a transatlantic crossing.

People in the south of England have bigger feet than northerners.

WHEN the occasional example of a two-tusked narwhal is found, both tusks invariably twist in the same direction, unlike goats and all other animals with twin spiral horns.

Tokyo and New York have restaurants for dogs.

IN 1925 the White House was fraudulently leased to a cattle rancher for 10,000 dollars.

ANCIENT Roman barbers dressed cuts with spiders' webs soaked in vinegar.

LONDONERS eat more fruit and fresh vegetables but less rhubarb than people in the provinces.

SAILORS wear gold earrings so that they always carry the cost of a Christian burial on their bodies.

A GALLUP poll revealed that the British idea of the perfect meal was the same in 1962 as in 1947: sherry, tomato soup, sole, roast chicken with roast potatoes, peas and sprouts. The only difference was in the dessert. In 1947 it was trifle and cream; by 1962, taste had moved on to fruit salad.

The fathom derives from an old English word meaning "outstretched arms"; fingertip to fingertip, an average man spans about 6 ft.

ADULT dolphins have a mental age equivalent to that of a child of seven.

Wrigley's make 853 million miles of chewing gum a year.

PRESIDENT Kaunda, a teetotaller, said he would resign if Zambians didn't stop drinking so much beer.

A GIRLS' boarding school at Fettan, Switzerland, had to be closed in the 1920s and the girls sent home for a fortnight to recover from general mania brought on by the unusual attractions of one of the female teaching staff.

IT was the height of fashion in the 17th century to tint the lips green or black.

In 1972, the Dartford Tunnel swallowed more than 25,000 cars. Although 4,787,092 vehicles left Kent for Essex, only 4,761,321 returned.

IN 1921, the year British women were given the vote, the Football Association banned ladies' soccer. Females were not officially allowed back on to the pitch until 1970.

THE Great Pyramid of Cheops contains more than five million tons of stone. It is 481 ft. high and covers more than 13 acres.

A NEW song craze swept San Francisco's six- and seven-year-olds. Sung to the tune of Frère Jacques: "Marijuana, Marijuana, LSD, LSD, Scientists make it, Teachers take it, Why can't we ? Why can't we ?"

THE ova of a blue whale, 0.1 to 0.2 mm. in diameter, are no bigger than those of a mouse.

BETWEEN the ages of 100 and 102, Mr James Chapman of Wisbech learned how to fly a Tiger Moth light aircraft, a hot-air balloon and a glider. He also learned to drive a combine harvester.

ARISTOTLE taught that while the more sophisticated members of the animal kingdom reproduced by mating, other less fortunate species grew spontaneously from mud and water.

Kashmiri working women change their clothes once a year, in spring.

A PARTICULARLY popular time to be woken by a telephone-call service in Paris is five o'clock in the afternoon.

MALTESE Joe Borg left 26 brothels to the Australian RSPCA.

THE erect penis of a rabbit flea, about a third as long as his body, is the most complicated of any animal.

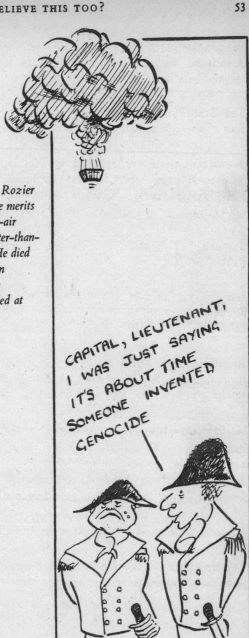

In 1785 Pilatre de Rozier tried to combine the merits of Montgolfier hot-air balloons with lighter-than-air gas balloons. He died when his hydrogen balloon with a fire underneath exploded at 3000 ft.

Studies in tedium: the Harvard Institute has found that the most boring job in the world is that of an assembly-line worker, followed by: lift operator, girl in typing pool, bank guard and housewife.

CAPTIVE squids suffering from depression commit suicide by eating their own tentacles.

BRITAIN'S chickens and geese produce six million tons of dung a year. Pigs can only manage one million but cows are responsible for a mighty 100 million tons annually, which could provide the same amount of gas as $2\frac{1}{2}$ million tons of oil.

BY ancient custom, when a Peruvian woman finds an unusually ugly potato she runs up to the nearest man and smashes it in his face.

A PARASITIC worm makes its home under a hippopotamus' eyelids and lives on tears.

Robert Spears, who
pleaded self-defence, was
acquitted of murdering a
man and throwing his
body into the Ohio River.
After the verdict he was
charged again, this time for
littering the river.

The younger generation of hedgehogs, twigging that their spines are a less than efficient protection against the motor car, are learning to cross roads at a safety-seeking gallop. Members of the old school, however, still stop dead at the thunder of pneumatic tyres and curl themselves into a ball.

A GIANT 10 times as heavy as an average man would break his leg every time he took a step unless his thigh-bone were so thickened as to be too heavy to move at all.

Eighteen of Britain's 46 Prime Ministers have been Old Etonians.

SEVEN thousand gas lamps were installed at St Paul's Cathedral for the Duke of Wellington's funeral in 1852 to create "an air of solemn and chastened magnificence".

HENRY VIII's armour has the largest codpiece in the Tower of London.

THE tail of the spider monkey is strong enough to hang by, and yet sensitive enough to probe for and pick up peanuts.

IN Ancient Britain the fine for insulting the King's bard was six cows and eight pence.

WHEN it was announced, in 1851, that a bathroom was to be installed in the White House, there was a public outcry against such unnecessary expenditure.

NEW 50p coins have a life expectancy of 50 years; the 10s notes they replaced lasted about six months.

A monkey washed ashore at Hartlepool, Co. Durham, during the Napoleonic Wars was mistaken by townsfolk for a French spy. The hapless animal was tried and hanged.

SO, MY PRETTY M'SIEU...
STILL YOU REFUSE
TO TALK!

ALL toothed whales are flesh-eaters except for a small dolphin that lives in the Cameroon River, West Africa.

TEN times more Mexicans die of scorpion stings than from snake-bites.

A PROFESSOR of semantics has distinguished 55 separate meanings of the word 'fascist'.

Britons spend three-and-a-half times as much on drinking and smoking as on life insurance.

JOSEPH di Pietro, of the USA, who set a bantamweight record by lifting 307.5 kg. at the London Olympics in 1948, was the shortest Olympic champion of all time. He stood just 4 ft. 8 in.

THERE are now more deer in southern England than at any time since Shakespeare's day.

A CHIMPANZEE called Pierre had many of his paintings sold and given serious critical comment before the hoax was discovered. Pierre was very highly strung and used to eat a banana a minute while in the process of creation.

GIVEN that one doggie year is one-seventh of a human year, canine coming-of-age should be celebrated after three years. An American poodle-owner did this by throwing a party for his pet and 29 pals; guests were offered diluted sherry, hors d'oeuvres, steak and vegetables, ice-cream and strawberry-flavoured milk served from champagne bottles.

THE giant squid has the biggest eye of any living creature, bigger than a man's head.

IN Britain the incomes of the richest 10 per cent are 15 times those of the poorest 10 per cent. America's rich are 29 times better off than its poor, and France's 76 times.

DURING the Middle Ages, corpses were often boiled to remove the flesh so that the bones could be transported more easily. Prepared for every eventuality, the Crusaders took their own cauldrons with them.

A FAKE wine was manufactured in Italy for 14 years before being detected. It was flavoured with dates, banana skins, carob pods and figs, clarified with lead acetate and neutralised with potassium.

Blushes are confined to the face of a clothed person, but spread right across a naked body.

Squire Mytton, who regularly drank a daily half-dozen bottles of port, found himself seized with hiccups after a particularly vigorous day's toping. Hoping to cure himself with a shock, he set fire to his nightshirt and burned to death.

THE Bank of England employs 50 patient souls whose job it is to identify tattered, sodden or burnt bits of paper as bank-notes.

One in every 2000 babies is born with teeth.

DURING the Middle Ages, Watling Street, Ermine Street, the Fosse Way and Icknield Way were regarded as royal roads; travellers were reckoned to be under the King's protection and anyone attacking them there was liable to a fine of 100s.

THE oldest fish on record was a sturgeon who lived in the Amsterdam Aquarium for 70 years.

A REFUSE collection company in Long Island, New York, has tanks and nozzles attached to its dustcarts from which to dispense perfume into clients' dustbins.

THE simplest way to escape from an angry bull is to run downhill. As the animal's front legs are shorter than its back legs, it can run faster uphill than down.

THE Berlin-Baghdad railway was started in 1888 and finished in 1940.

ITEMS considered by the Cornwall Hospital Management Committee under the heading "losses and compensations" included a set of false teeth, 50 patients' X-ray gowns, a condemned sheep and a watch damaged in a struggle with a patient.

TWO minor earthquakes happen every minute.

A GERMAN psychiatric team concluded that classical musicians are generally well-adjusted. But they found that 82 per cent of modern musicians are nervous, 81 per cent are irritable, 62 per cent are quarrelsome, 39 per cent suffer from insomnia and 22 per cent have headaches. It was found that modern musicians who turned to the classics "began to feel better".

As a boy, Clive of India ran a protection racket, extorting money from shopkeepers in his home town of Market Drayton.

CLARENCE Birdseye got the idea of selling frozen food after dining with natives of Labrador on caribou which had been frozen in the Arctic ice.

LEGEND has it that Scotland adopted the thistle as its national emblem after a member of a Danish force marching on Stirling Castle trod on one and let out a yell that warned the defenders of their approach.

Every British Post Office is entitled to an official cat on the payroll at a wage of between $17\frac{1}{2}$p and 35p, depending on the number of mice to be caught.

Henry III of France liked to walk the streets of Paris with a basket of puppies round his neck.

THERE are about 150,000 stray dogs in New York City.

The octopus has three hearts.

A JOURNALIST who went to interview the Boston Strangler in jail was denied access to his subject until he had first been home and put on a tie.

BREAKFAST for Count Apraxine, a frequent guest at the Hotel de Cap d'Antibes at the turn of the century, was a dozen fresh, out-of-season strawberries, costing a gold sovereign each. He would carefully mash them to a pulp, and then return them to the kitchen uneaten.

WHEN Fred Finn died, a life insurance claim for 5000 dollars was filed. Only then did the company spot what their computer had disregarded when issuing the policy—that Finn's height was registered as 3 cm. and his weight 0.3 g. After a legal wrangle, the company paid out 650 dollars to the owner of Fred the goldfish.

TARANTULAS can live for two and a half years without food.

THE parking meter was invented by Mr C. C. Magee in 1935.

THE chilling tale of the sheep-liver fluke: life starts by hatching inside a snail, from which it is ejected in a ball of slime. These balls are eaten by ants, but the fluke works its way through the ant's body until it reaches the brain where, by manipulating the nerves, it takes control of the ant, by now a robot vehicle. Under the command of the fluke, the ant climbs to the tip of blade of grass or weed where, hopefully, it is munched by a passing sheep. From the sheep's stomach, the flukes makes its journey home—to the liver.

Inconvenience caused by traffic jams in England costs almost as much as the sum collected annually in road tax.

DURING the Second World War the Natural History Museum moved its unique collection of pickled snakes to the safety of some Surrey caves.

In 1714 the British Government offered a prize of £20,000 for a method of determining longitude to within half a degree. They had been studying the problem without success ever since a fleet commanded by Sir Cloudesley Shovel lost its way and collided with the Scilly Isles.

IN 1968 a London hairdresser sold wigs for poodles ranging in price from 8 gns to 21 gns; the going rate for a poodle shampoo and set is 2 gns.

THERE are 93,000 acres of officially derelict land in England.

EVEN averagely insensitive fingers can detect the difference between a flat pane of glass and one with grooves 1/2500 in. deep.

BOTTOM'S DROPPED RIGHT OUT OF THE MARKET SINCE MARKS AND SPARKS OPENED IN THE HIGH STREET.

JOAN & BETT
LADIES' GEAR

CLOSING DOWN SALE

ALL HALF PRICE

SAVE ON KNIX

Two of every three British women wear Marks & Spencer's knickers.

WHEN the conservationists' battle to save the London Coal Exchange building failed, the city of Melbourne offered to pay for it to be shipped to Australia. The London authorities, insisting that there was no time to lose, refused. The site is now a car park.

IF they all survived and multiplied, at the end of a year the descendants of one aphid would weigh as much as 600 million men.

SOME dog food manufacturers have tried to enhance the appeal of their wares by adding synthetic colouring. Dogs are colour-blind.

THE going price for an Indonesian girl sold into prostitution is 1300 dollars for a virgin and 875 dollars for a once-married woman.

A coprophagist eats dung; an anthropophagist eats men; a lithophagist eats stones.

THE white cliffs of Dover are retreating from France at the rate of up to 15 in. a year.

Ten cows would belch enough gas to provide the heating for a small house.

THE 'juke' in juke-box comes from the Old English word 'jouk', meaning 'to dance'.

EVIAN, the French spa, has a healing spring for dogs only.

DR Keate, a headmaster of Eton College, commanded his pupils to be pure in heart, "for if not I'll flog you until you are". He once publicly flogged 80 boys in a day and, when he died in 1852, he'd had the distinction of administering the birch to half the bishops, generals and dukes in the kingdom.

THE push-button toilet is one Australian invention.

No rain has ever been recorded in the Atacama Desert in Chile.

AN English couple employed a chauffeur to drive an estate car for their two 14 st. St Bernard dogs.

Britain has two sheep for every human.

WHILE drinking at his London club, Squire Fuller bet a friend that he could see seven church spires from his country house. On his return home, however, there were only six in view. Undaunted, he had a seventh spire built on a nearby hill.

DURING the 1860s, fashion-conscious ladies wore hats made of whole stuffed pheasants or grouse.

In 1970, teachers at a primary school near Barnsley, Yorkshire, found that some children could not eat their school dinners with knives and forks as they had been accustomed to eating only fish and chips out of the paper.

OH VERY WELL, IF YOU DON'T LIKE YOUR SEMOLINA JUST LEAVE IT IN THE MARGIN

People who don't smoke are heavier dreamers than those who do.

THE Bide-a-wee Home Association Inc. provides a pension plan for pets, offering canine and feline geriatrics a warm and comfortable retirement on Long Island.

A SPECIES of sea-weed found in the Pacific has been known to reach a length of 600 ft.

In 1972 the British drank enough whisky to fill 25 public swimming pools.

BRITISH sausages were refused entry to the 1958 Brussels World Fair because they did not contain enough meat.

KASMAN Fashions were fined £100 for a breach of the Trades Descriptions Act when a disappointed customer complained that the set of "funwear" black leather underwear he had ordered for his wife turned out to be made of plastic.

AN 82-year-old Ukrainian woman found her long-lost wedding ring inside the 1973 Christmas turkey. The diamond-and-gold ring slipped from her finger while she was working on the family farm in 1914.

DRIZZLE droplets are about one-fiftieth of an inch in width, fog droplets about one-thousandth of an inch, and raindrops (maximum speed 18 m.p.h.) about a fifth of an inch.

There are 2300 man-made objects in orbit around the earth, ranging from spent rockets to lost spanners.

PERPETUAL motion is no mystery to rabbits, who eat their own soft faecal pellets produced underground. They do not eat the unappetising hard pellets produced outside the burrow, of which each animal leaves about 360 each day.

A London solicitor named Robinson patented in 1895 a method for using the heat from street gas-lamps to provide hot water, cocoa, coffee and beef tea.

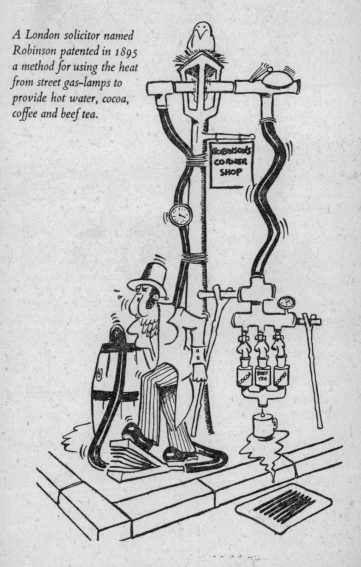

The parish register at Lymington shows that in 1736 Samuel Baldwin was buried at sea. The ceremony was performed at the deceased's own request to disappoint his wife, who in frequent squabbles had declared her intention to dance on his grave.

A FREAK storm showered more than 100,000 small toads on the village of Brignoles, France.

Thieves in London have a turnover of about £1 per second.

THE Bumble bee is technically too heavy to fly.

A MONKEY in Chile which went berserk after eating a hot pepper sandwich was taken to court and sentenced to life imprisonment in a local zoo.

WHEN consumers were asked to give their verdicts on the coffee in a range of different packs, 73 per cent said the coffee in a dark brown pack was too strong; 84 per cent said a red pack was "richer"; 79 per cent said a blue pack was "milder"; and 87 per cent said a yellow pack was "too weak". All the packs contained identical coffee.

AN ELDERLY gentleman applying for car insurance admitted to three accidents: once his car had been hit by an aircraft, once rammed by a yacht and once swamped by a giant wave.

THE world's first unsuccessful airborne stowaway was discovered on Laurentide Air Services' maiden flight between Rouyn and Haileybury, Canada, in 1924.

Between 60,000 and 70,000 bodies were buried in a 200 ft. square plot of St. Martin-in-the-Fields in the mid-19th century.

MPs drink 2500 pints of beer in the House of Commons every week.

PRE-PROHIBITION New York City had about 15,000 saloons; within a year of the Volstead Act there were more than twice that number of speak-easies in the city.

ST Peter's, Rome, would fit inside Europe's biggest cave, the Grotto dei Giganti near Trieste.

Dolphins can detect a shirt button at the bottom of a tank even when blindfolded.

A 78-seater bus does 546 passenger miles to the gallon when full, 437 when 80 per cent full, and 66 when 12 per cent full.

AFTER the world fishing exhibition at Vigo, Spain, in 1973, thousands of dead fish suddenly appeared in the harbour. They had been killed by the detergent used to clean up the exhibition site.

BRITISH women high-jumpers finished second in every Olympic Games between 1936 and 1960.

HOT and cold running water was pioneered by the first Duke of Devonshire.

MORAL purists in the Middle Ages felt that, since the Virgin Mary had conceived through her ear, women's ears should be kept covered as if they were sex organs.

No insurance company has yet dared offer third-party cover for a nuclear power station.

Nosmo King, the British music-hall artist, hit upon his stage name when he walked through a pair of swing doors bearing the instruction No Smoking.

TWO years after narrowly missing a gold medal in the marathon at the 1964 Tokyo Olympics, Japanese athlete Kokichi Tsubmaya committed hara-kiri for failing his country.

SIX people died in the Mbeya region of Tanzania after drinking insecticide. A government official said the victims believed the poison would cure them of worms.

It is an offence to slam a car door in Switzerland.

CHARLES Osborn, of Iowa, hiccupped continuously for more than 50 years after trying to lift 25 st. pig in 1922.

THE 15th-century fashion for square-ended shoes was launched by King Charles VIII of France. He had six toes on one foot.

IN 1973 a dog made £9000 in four months on the London Stock Exchange. What rankled most with less successful human punters was that he paid no tax on his profits.

AN Australian colonel in 1973 paid £70 for a slice of Queen Victoria's wedding cake.

THE remains of 343 earwigs were found in a single regurgitated owl pellet.

A British holiday-maker involved in an Arab attack on Athens airport reported: "At one point they threatened to take us to Saudi Arabia. I never believed anything like this could happen on a charter booking."

At wedding ceremonies in the Black Forest, at St Georgen, the happy couple try to tread on each other's toes; traditionally, the first to succeed will dominate the marriage.

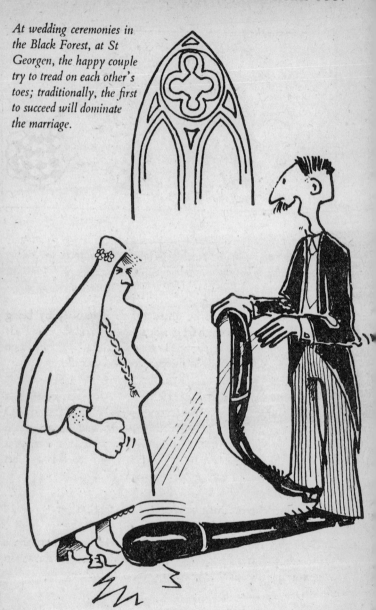

Clowns protect the copyright of their styles of make-up by painting the design on eggshells stored in the vaults of the International Circus Club in Paris.

BRITISH bulldogs used to be tested for their ferocity by being made to hang by their teeth from a horizontal wooden pole. Their hind legs would then be chopped off and the dog which held on the longest would be judged the best breeding stock.

ON the first night of the opera *Charles VI* in Paris in 1849, a member of the company died on stage at the start of the aria "O God, Kill Him!" The next night the same aria signalled the death by apoplexy of one of the audience. When, on the third night at the same time, the leader of the orchestra suffered a fatal heart attack, Napoleon III banned further performances.

St Vincent, patron saint of wine, was a teetotaller.

IN December 1963 a Florida police patrol picked up a chimpanzee for speeding. It was a hoax, however: a hidden carnival showman was working the pedals; the chimp was only steering.

FIFTY-TWO per cent of Australians told pollsters they were "very happy". Britain notched up a creditable 39 per cent, but France could muster only 11 per cent.

There are no South American apes.

RESEARCH in the USA suggests that breast-fed babies, even if sleeping in separate rooms, dream in unison with their mothers.

THE first contender at a drinking contest at Wroxham, Norfolk, in 1810 downed 44½ pints of porter in 55 minutes. His opponent countered with 52½ pints in the same time, took two more pints for good measure and, declaring himself sober as a judge, rowed six miles home.

IN 1973 Idi Amin took delivery of 1201 Royal Stewart tartan kilts: 1200 for the 50 pipe bands he had created in the Ugandan Army; the other for himself.

A WHOLESOME lass whose photograph, nuzzling an infant, was used to encourage mums to buy a certain brand of soap powder, later delighted the dads—and caused consternation among the manufacturers—by starring in a hard-core porn movie in which she entertained four men on a trapeze.

IF you tried to visit every one of the 6700 museums in North America at the rate of one a day, it would take you more than 18 years. By then another 4700 would have opened, which would occupy another 13 years or so. And by then . . .

A MEMBER who failed to attend the Shopkeepers' Guild annual dinner at the Guild Hall in the 14th century had to pay a fine of ½ lb. of wax.

The kiwi is the same size as a domestic hen but lays an egg eight times as big.

The first crossword puzzle was published by the "Sunday Express" in 1924.

A survey carried out by a wig-maker revealed that 51 per cent of male hairpiece-wearers think their false thatch gives them more sex appeal. More than a third think it improves their performance in bed.

HOMER and Langley Collyer filled their New York house with rubbish and protected it with booby-traps. When neither had been seen for sometime in the spring of 1947, police investigators soon found Langley—dead in bed. But to find Homer, who had been killed by one of his own booby-traps, they had to tunnel through the house for 19 days, removing more than 100 tons of newspaper, thousands of cardboard boxes and rags, furniture, pieces of cars, five violins and 17 pianos.

To carry one extra pound of payload on a moonflight requires an extra 2,590 lb. of fuel.

BETWEEN now and 1980, nine new supermarkets are expected to open in Britain every week.

THE standard acquisitive U.S. male spends 17 per cent of his life on his car—driving it, parking it, cleaning it, and earning enough to run it. In return the loved one boosts his lifetime average speed, from cradle to grave, to 4 m.p.h.

WHEN the Pope visited Bogotá, capital of Colombia, all the women fitted with IUDs packed into the Profamilia family planning clinic to have them devoutly removed. No-one visited the clinic while the Pope was in town, but the day after he left it had the busiest day in its history, putting everything back again.

Juke boxes in America frequently offer, for the sensitive minority, three minutes of recorded silence.

IN the Middle Ages, 1 lb. of ginger was worth a sheep, and 1 lb. of mace was worth three sheep or half a cow.

CHORLEYWOOD, in Hertfordshire, is the most highly motorised place in Britain. There are 123 cars for every 100 homes.

COFFINS intended for use at cremations in Britain are fitted with inflammable plastic handles.

COMMERCIAL jam pips are often made from wood.

THE great-great-grandson of a soldier who fought at the Battle of Waterloo claimed £20 that was owed to his ancestor by the British Army. If the missing money had been invested at 10 per cent in 1915 it would now be worth about £69 million.

MAN, the higher apes, the guinea pig, the fruit bat and the red-vented bul-bul bird are the only species for whom vitamin C is essential for good health.

More than 1000 million fish fingers are eaten in Britain every year.

ELM Farm Ollie was the first cow to fly. The milk she produced during an air-trip in 1930 was dropped by parachute over the city of St Louis.

FOR 36 years, the only memorial to the gallant pigeons who braved German bullets and hawks to carry messages in and out of a besieged Paris in 1870 was an epic poem entitled *Les Pigeons de la République*. The callous authorities had disposed of the few surviving birds for a franc apiece, but made amends for their ingratitude by erecting a statue in 1906.

The Greek Council of State awarded a full pension to the widow of a seaman who died while committing adultery in the Philippines; his fatal heart attack was judged to be a work accident.

A MAN with a healthy liver is capable of drinking half a pint of beer an hour indefinitely without getting drunk.

The teddy bear was named after President Theodore Roosevelt. He started the fashion for bears when he adopted one as a pet during a hunting expedition to the Rockies. An alert Brooklyn stationer began immediately to manufacture toy bears and wrote to the President for permission to use the name Teddy. Roosevelt replied: "I don't think my name is likely to be worth much in the bear business, but you are welcome to use it". Since then, more than 150 million teddy bears have been sold all over the world.

AT a Southampton shipyard 200 electricians went on strike when one of their number was sacked and six suspended after being found on board a Naval frigate watching a blue movie called *Belle Bottoms*.

BEREAVED Victorian girls married in black bridal gowns.

AT the end of the 19th century, New South Wales offered 12 alternative ways of disposing of the dead. There were six different sorts of earth burial: surface burial, tree burial, exposure to the air, burning, smoking and eating.

A GREENGROCER was compensated by his insurance company after his Labrador ate £80 in notes from the day's takings.

IN pre-war Japan, the personage of the Emperor was too sacrosanct to be touched. Even his tailor had respectfully to estimate the imperial dimensions at a distance of several yards.

A ROSE by any other name: Mr J. W. G. Musty is an Inspector of Ancient Monuments, Dr J. M. Looney is a psychiatrist, Miss Mercedes Concepción works in population control, Mr G. C. Cheesman is employed by the Institute of Dairying and Mr Zacharia Ovary is a gynaecologist.

A PASSING fashion in France was to wear earrings of tiny, live South American snakes tethered to gold clips.

A dam—as in the phrase "I don't give a dam"—was a small Indian coin.

A BOOKSHOP in the fashionable London suburb of Hampstead, in an effort to reduce shop-lifting, pinned up the notice: "Children of progressive parents not admitted."

A 15th-century law forbade all but the nobility to carry hand-kerchiefs.

The French eat 600 million snails every year. Laid antennae to tail they would stretch round the Equator one and a half times.

WHEN the white population of Minnesota rose from 6077 in 1850 to an estimated 150,000 seven years later, the inhabitants of the main town, Pig's Eye, voted that its name should be changed to St Paul.

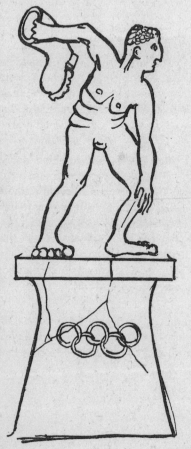

The Olympic Acceptance Board received an application from the Gumboot Olympic Committee for recognition of their sport. Their spokesman was Australian Ron Payton, holder of the Silver Welly, who had pitched a gumboot 111.3 ft., beating the previous world record by an inch.

Some hotels in Las Vegas have swimming pools furnished with floating gambling tables.

AN AMERICAN woman tourist hired a car to drive from London to Cornwall. She complained to an A.A. patrolman afterwards that the engine roared, lights kept flashing, she could not reach 50 m.p.h. and had used 54 gallons of petrol to cover 200 miles. The patrolman found she had driven the whole way in second gear.

A 19-YEAR-OLD Memphis housewife claimed a million dollars damages against a health spa where, she said, an hour-and-a-half trapped inside a sauna bath had turned her from a devout Catholic into an insatiable nymphomaniac. Appearing before a grand jury investigating a vice wave in Memphis, the lady admitted that she'd had carnal knowledge of 5000 police officers of all ranks during a three-year period. Asked why she made a speciality of policemen, she said she thought it must have had something to do with her belief in law and order.

INHABITANTS of Mabaan villages in the Sudan live with a noise level roughly equivalent to that of a public library. Tests showed that Mabaan men between 70 and 79 had better hearing than Americans between 30 and 39.

The only meat available to Olympic competitors at St Louis in 1904 was buffalo.

A BULLDOG in Nuremburg was found guilty of biting a policeman and its owner was fined £35. The ferocious beast had only one tooth.

THE Canadian Air Force has lost five Starfighter jets in collisions with birds.

KIWIS are the only birds to hunt by smell.

WHEN a memorandum about paper-saving was circularised at the University of Durham, six copies were sent to the Department of Archaeology and nine to the Department of Classics.

JAMES Holman, who lost his sight in 1810, was later expelled from Russia on suspicion of spying.

Mrs E. M. Hull, who wrote "The Sheik" the romantic vehicle for Rudolph Valentino, was married to a pig-breeder named Percy.

WAVES on the sea break when their height is more than seven-tenths of the depth of the water.

WHEN coyness struck the Roman Catholic Church, statues all over Italy had their manhood replaced with fig leaves. A Vatican curator now guards a secret cellar stacked high with stone genitalia.

THE star of a film called *I am Frigid* was billed in London's Charing Cross Road as "Sandra Jullien, of *I am a Nymphomaniac*".

IN honour of the soldiers who saved the town in 1917, Dainville, near Arras, has a street named Rue de London Scottish Regiment.

A LONDON restaurant attracted the attentions of the public health authorities by putting Rat Terrine on the menu. The resourceful caterer said he obtained his supply of rats "out in the back yard".

AN 18th-century American trapper could get 50 cents for a doe-skin, but twice that for a buck's—hence the expression 'buck' for a dollar.

EACH Briton consumes an average of 2 lb. of sugar every week, and 50 cwt. in a lifetime.

WAGNER wore pink underwear.

THE fashion for ladies of the Egyptian court to wear beehive hairstyles and polish their heads to achieve a smooth, elongated profile, was begun by Nefertiti's six daughters, whose heads were narrowed by doctors during birth to minimise their mother's labour pains.

Tiger-shooting is sometimes made easier for visiting dignitaries and rich tourists in India by lacing the animals' water-holes with opium.

American Indians have a neat way of naming their children. After taking his first look at the newborn baby, the father steps outside and names the child after the first thing he sees. Hence Flying Cloud, Laughing Water, Sitting Bull, etc.

In 1973 a British cub scout won a proficiency badge for snooker.

IF A party of 13 arrives for dinner at London's Savoy Hotel, an extra place is laid for Kaspar the cat.

THE Swiss eat more cheese per head than any other nation.

IT has been scientifically proved that a good hangover cure is another drink.

WINDOWS in Hawaiian hotels are double-glazed to keep out the sound of mynah birds.

Dolphins sleep for only two hours a day. So do elephants.

JEAN-CLAUDE Dague was imprisoned in France for seven bank robberies. M Dague turned to crime in order to finance gangster films.

Clarkstown, New Jersey, appointed a 60-year-old blind man to be its chief cinema censor.

A GUNMAN who tried to hold up the Post Office at Chard, in France, was thwarted by the success of his disguise—his enormous false nose made the cashier laugh so loudly that he took fright and ran off empty-handed. .

POMEGRANATES were successfully grown in England in 1933 and 1949.

Two murderers have confessed, six alcoholics have renounced drink and 300 people have been christened at a Japanese coffee shop run by Chinese Christians.

BEER gushed from domestic taps in Bydgoszc, Poland, when a faulty valve at a brewery diverted ale into the city's water mains.

Tourists in Zambia face arrest and severe punishment if caught taking photographs of pygmies.

THE publicity office at the London Hilton Hotel explains that the bright green carpet in the Olde Englishe Tavern is intended to "suggest the green of the English countryside".

According to the Mayans of Central America, time began in 3113 B.C.

PLASTIC funeral wreaths are such good sellers in the United States that they are stocked in supermarkets.

British law can compel anyone who demolishes a protected historic building to re-erect it.

HMM.. DEATH BY BRICKLAYING...

For pet-owning without fear a chastity belt is marketed for dogs.
Called Petnix, it allows petting but not mating.

THE winner of the annual worm championship races in California is the first competitor to cover a circle with a 3 ft. radius.

AT the Congress of Vienna, shortly after the Battle of Waterloo, the only uncontested resolution passed by the allies was that Brie deserved the title of King of Cheeses.

THE orang-utan's warning signal is a loud belch.

IN a single year 3647 Americans with access to nuclear weapons got the sack. Twenty per cent were dismissed for drug abuse, the rest for disciplinary problems, alcoholism or mental illness.

A PUFFIN eats the equivalent of its own body-weight in 24 hours.

THE Chinese used fingerprints for identification in A.D. 700.

A San Francisco park has the world's only human juke box. You put your coin in a slot and press a selector button in the usual way. But instead of an impersonal plastic disc, a lid opens, out pops a trumpeter to play the tune of your choice, after which he smiles pleasantly and disappears back into his box.

IN ENGLAND's southern suburbs, each milk bottle makes an average of 50 trips before being lost or broken. In Glasgow the average is six. The national average in 1960 was 45 trips; today it is 25.

AFRICAN municipal bus drivers in Springs, Johannesburg, get a bonus each month if they refrain from attacking passengers.

A GULLIBLE American in the 1920s paid £6000 for Nelson's Column.

BEFORE the 13th century, the use of buttons to fasten your clothing was taken as an indication that you led a loose life.

A YOUNG wife was granted a nullity decree in the London Divorce Court because her spouse was "not a man". The judge commented that there seemed to have been quite serious deceit.

MOURNERS in the south of England prefer to bury their loved ones in coffins with brass handles, while their northern and Welsh counterparts more usually opt for nickel. The northerner, more-over, actually uses the handles to carry the coffin; the southerner supports the box on his shoulders.

An American child need be only a moderate television viewer to have been exposed to 80,000 commercials by the age of 16.

WHEN the chief cashier of the Bank of England was directed to attend High Court proceedings to recover blocked Rhodesian moneys a solicitor handed to him, as is required by law, his 10p bus fare from the Bank to the Court.

BIRDS are adept at parasitology. They plaster ants to their feathers so that the formic acid in the insects' bodies will poison other unwanted guests.

LESS than a quarter of one per cent of the liquid content of perfume aerosols is actually perfume.

A MALE convict at America's San Quentin jail filed a suit in a U.S. district court, demanding the removal of two women prison guards because their proximity constituted "cruel and unusual punishment".

An Indian maharajah has a bed guarded at each corner by a realistic life-size nude robot. His weight triggers off a musical box and the mechanical ladies fan his face and feet in time to the music.

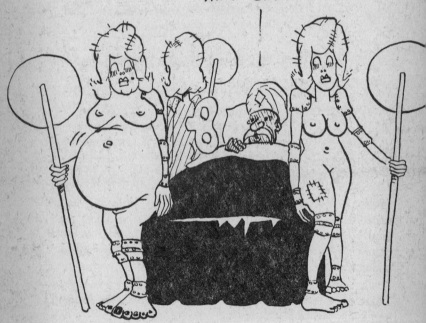

When the Bancroft House hotel opened in Saginaw, Michigan, in 1879, all the local millionaires were invited to a grand opening banquet except arriviste Curt Emerson. Just as the chosen few began tucking into terrapin à la Maryland, Emerson suddenly appeared, leapt screaming on to the long table and kicked his way from one end to the other, sending dishes and guests flying. Next day he paid the hotel 2000 dollars compensation, but he was never omitted from a guest list again.

WHEN Jacques Ferron was hanged in 1750 for having had unnatural relations with a donkey, several citizens (including the local abbot) spoke up for the previous good character of his mount. The court acquitted the donkey, declaring that she had undoubtedly been the victim of rape.

There are enough zips in the world to reach to the moon and back, twice.

SNAKES have two sets of genitals. Some have been seen to take twenty-two hours to complete copulation.

TO SAVE £21,000 a year, the City of London Common Council closed six gentlemen's and three ladies' lavatories. The chairman of the Planning Committee explained: "Observations have been kept of the various conveniences and a list of people who frequented them."

THE most expensive portion of chicken and aspic in the world may well have been the one Nubar Gulbenkian charged up to his father Calouste's expense account. The resulting lawsuit between them cost £50,000 in barristers' fees alone.

Men use 2.7 calories of energy per minute when peeling potatoes, but women only 1.29.

DURING a two-week trip, 13 locomotives drew Lincoln's funeral train 1700 miles past seven million watchers.

ANIMAL hospitals in the USA are increasing three times as fast as human hospitals.

THE British Army abandoned the lance as an operational weapon in 1927.

IN THE Middle Ages a rabbit was worth sixpence but a pig only fourpence.

MAIL addressed to Sherlock Holmes, 22A Baker Street, London, W1, is always answered. The insurance company now occupying the building employs someone full-time to deal with Holmes's correspondence.

*Specially high standpipes have been developed to replenish water
bags on camels' backs.*

RHUBARB was introduced to Europe by Marco Polo, who brought it back from the court of the Chinese emperor Kublai Khan.

A DISTINGUISHED doctor, called to Buckingham Palace during a London bomb-alert, was stopped at the gate by guardsmen who asked to search the boot of his Fiat 500. The soldiers took one look at the contents—the engine—and ran for cover.

STEEL may be hardened by contact with nitrogen. Several hundred years ago, before the availability of the liquid gas, red hot swords were treated by being plunged into prisoners.

> *The skin of rorqual whales has no commercial value, but whalers often used the dried skin of the penis to make golf bags. A blue whale bag is recognisable by its creamy white colour and blue-grey stripes; a fin whale bag is unflecked white.*

WHITELAW REID, millionaire owner of a massive country estate near Sing Sing prison, used to keep a couple of old suits hanging on a barn near the road, for the convenience of escaped convicts.

THE Victorians devised strict rules governing mourning. For a widow, the transition from deep mourning, in black crepe-covered dress and mantle, through the various stages of 'slighting' and half-mourning, when grey or lavender was permitted, took two-and-a-half years. For a parent or child 12 months would suffice. Grandparents, brothers and sisters were valued at six months only.

After a Test match in Melbourne, the groundsmen picked up 30,000 empty beer cans.

THE Empress Poppaea, Nero's wife, had 500 milk asses to keep her bath topped up.

THE word 'gear' was used for clothes at least as early as 1549.

EVERY pint of Dead Sea contains 4 oz. of salt.

ARMADILLOS zealously mark out their territory with urine. In early zoos where their cages were cleaned out too often, many of them died of dehydration.

THE automatic telephone dialling system was invented by an undertaker.

AMONG the towns near Pennsylvania inhabited by the God-fearing Amish people, notable for their refusal to use any machine —even buttons—are Paradise, Intercourse and Fertility.

Following its success at
raising attendances in the
Sunday School, a 4 ft. 9 in.
robot, with a voice like a
Dalek and red eyes which
flash as it speaks, was
introduced to read the
lessons during adult
services at the Elim
Pentecostal Church,
Nottingham.

EIGHT candidates ran for Mayor in Camden, New Jersey, in 1973. One had served 15 years for murder; another had been convicted of assault and battery; a third had been arrested for threatening to kill; and a fourth had a string of convictions ranging from fraud to larceny.

THE plump patrons of Dame Trot, an 11th-century doctor of the School of Salerno, slimmed with the aid of friction rubs made with cow dung dissolved in good wine. They removed super-fluous hair with quicklime, whitened their skin with leeches, bleached their hair with calf's kidneys and softened it by rubbing the scalp with the body of a lizard boiled in olive oil.

ANGLO-SAXONS thought Friday so unlucky that any child born on that day was killed rather than be allowed to grow up to a life of misfortune.

Four people have jumped off the Eiffel Tower every year since it was built in 1889.

MRS Ethel Murphy booked a taxi to take her from Horsham, Sussex, to Perth, Australia. "When you're going that far," she said, "it's silly to rush it by jet and see nothing." The fare, not counting a tip, came to £1500.

AN Elizabethan lady's court dress cost the equivalent of between £2000 and £4000.

Bakelite was first used to make the gear knob for Rolls-Royces.

AT a rate of one second per person, it would take more than a century to count the population of the world.

IN an eight-hour working day the average American spends one hour earning enough to pay his rent, 58 minutes to buy his food, and two hours 39 minutes to pay his taxes.

AT the beginning of 1974, interest rates in Britain were precisely equivalent to those which the bankrupt Philip II of Spain had to pay after the loss of the Armada.

PHILIPPE LE BEL forbade his medieval French dukes, counts, barons and their ladies to own more than four garments each. Unmarried women were permitted only one dress unless they had inherited a castle.

TOP British marbles team, the Toucan Terribles, grind their own marbles out of lavatory bowls.

DURING a game of seven-card stud in the Sahara Hotel, Las Vegas, two players were dealt royal straight flushes in the same hand, against odds of about one billion to one.

The Ancient Egyptians were devoted to their pets. When a beloved cat died they shaved off their eyebrows as a sign of mourning. When a dog died, they shaved their whole body.

ON the occasion of H.E. The Viceroy's birthday on December 31, 1931, the Indian Air Mail Society and Calcutta Homing Pigeon Club sent birdborne air letters inscribed: "PIGEONGRAM—A MESSAGE FOR 1932 FROM HIS EXCELLENCY THE VICEROY—HONESTY IS THE BEST POLICY."

CHINESE diplomats are left in no doubt about the proper way to behave at the alien Western ritual of the cocktail party. Chairman Mao's little red book of etiquette lays down that Second Secretaries may drink up to three glasses of 90 per cent proof Mao Tai. More senior diplomats can have up to 15 glasses but the Ambassador, on his sober pinnacle of responsibility, is allowed only one.

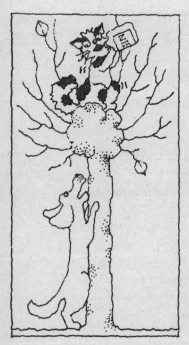

Cats under stress develop a taste for alcohol.

WILLIAM Shakespeare left his second-best bed to his wife.

A TEACHER in a small Czechoslovakian town, afraid that his school would close for lack of children, took it upon himself to spend four years sneaking around the houses after dark knocking on the windows of young married couples to keep them awake. The school is still in business.

Queen Victoria had a handkerchief embroidered with tear-drops for use in mourning.

THE fairy tern lays its eggs in the bare forks of trees.

The Royal Navy beer ration in 1590 was a gallon a day for each sailor. In 1731 they were offered the option of a pint of wine or half a pint of rum.

JOSEPH Berkas was given an absolute discharge after he had explained to a court in Vienna why he had rushed into the bed-room of his landlady's 21-year-old daughter, ripped away the towel with which she was covering herself and made a close, fingertip examination of her bottom. A keen philatelist, he said he had left a valuable foreign stamp soaking in the bathtub. And it had disappeared.

More than three million Americans buy hot meals from slot machines every day.

BETWEEN 1852 and 1872 Mary Ann Cotton, a life-assurance enthusiast, murdered three husbands, 15 children, a lodger and her mother with a mixture of arsenic and soft soap. For good measure, she pushed a boyfriend down a mineshaft. Just before she was hanged she confessed she had "done" the poisoning, but it was more of an accident than anything.

THE actor who played the part of Superman on television needed three men to help him out of his costume.

LOCAL health officials were faced with a seemingly insoluble disposal problem when the body of a 50 ft. whale appeared on a Lincolnshire beach. But the obliging monster solved their dilemma by spontaneously exploding.

A NOTICE in a hotel in Avallon, France, requested: "Please don't lay any stranger bodys in the W.C."

WHEN Paul Soglin, a former student activist with an arrest record for disturbing the peace, made a bid to become Mayor of Madison, Wisconsin, a local newspaper ran the headline "Radical Runs for Mayor". When Soglin won, the same paper headlined its report "Ex-radical Elected Mayor".

THE Houses of Parliament cover eight acres, have more than 1000 rooms, over 100 staircases and two miles of passages.

WHEN Idi Amin created the Order of the Mosquito to be awarded for civil or military gallantry, he said he was honouring the insect as a reward for its key role in inhibiting European settlement in Uganda.

FLAT out, a sloth can move twice as fast through water as it can overland. Its maximum swimming speed is one mile in four hours.

IN PORTUGAL during the 16th century there were twice as many glove perfumers, and three times as many cosmetics experts, as there were teachers.

In 1912, London's 2500 buses were driven so recklessly that they killed one pedestrian every two days.

A Band of Hope tract published for children in 1900 gave this
summary of "The History of Drinking in England": Britons and
Romans—Occasionally intemperate; Saxons and Danes—Great
drinkers; Normans—Copied English intemperance; Plantagenets—
Lived luxuriously; Tudors—Intemperance increased; Stuarts—
Wild excesses; Hanoverians—Drunkenness became A National
Vice.

A NEWCOMER to the ranks of religious literature in the United
States is entitled *Zen and the Art of Motorcycle Maintenance.*

To CONFUSE evil spirits, who could fly only in straight lines, the
Chinese built their houses with rounded corners.

JESSE Varley, an accountant-clerk with Wolverhampton Education Department, bolstered his salary in 1915-16 by inventing 155 fictitious assistant teachers to add to the 138 genuinely on the borough's books. Within a year he had increased his £325 annual pay by £14,000—equivalent to a borough rate of 8½d in the pound, and adding 17 per cent to the borough's total expenditure. He was unmasked when an office junior noticed that salaries were being paid to a dead teacher.

The 10 per cent of Britons who live in Scotland get through 20 per cent of the nation's whisky.

A HERD of wild wallabies lives in Derbyshire.

AFTER banquets at Buckingham Palace, the dirty plates are returned to the kitchen in leather buckets to avoid scratching the gold.

Paradichlorobenzene, once a popular ant-killer, is now commonly used in deodorants.

To demonstrate successes in battle, Ethiopian warriors used to snip off their victims' testicles and suspend them from their lances.

DURING the 19th century bereaved Cornish families decked their bird cages and pot-plants in mourning. They were outmourned, however, by the French, who hung black drapery on everything from trees to pigsties and the farmyard cat.

GENERAL Motors' £10,000 million turnover is 120 times greater than that of America's 10 top black-owned corporations added together.

BIRTH control projects in Asia achieved remarkable success when multi-coloured condoms were introduced.

IN 1962 the average British man spent £73 on cigarettes and 12s. 6d. (62½p) on a bed.

THE first weaving looms in Bristol were established in 1337 by Thomas Blanket.

The average housewife walks four miles and spends 25 hours a year making one bed.

EIGHTY-NINE people died during a four-day carnival in Rio de Janeiro. Causes of death were alcoholic poisoning, road accidents and heart attacks. There were also 47 murders.

A HINDU should not die in bed, but on the ground and preferably beside a river. If he dies on the floor, the area should first have been washed with a solution of cow dung.

CANDIDATES for the 1966 University of London GCE O-level examinations in English and Mathematics included Messrs. Goodtidings Sunday Harry, Festus Silvanius Theophilus Thorpe, Sixpence Mbokwe and Pockets Mgugu.

The first aircraft to shoot itself down was an American F14 fighter in Vietnam, using a Sparrow air-to-air missile.

To flavour 100 lb. of boiled sweets you need 30 lb. of natural strawberry juice—or ½ oz. of artificial flavouring.

ICE-CREAM owes much of its flavour to wood-pulp and soft drinks are often sweetened with coal.

THE Brazilian Embassy in London has the car registration number BRA 1; the manager of a ladies' underwear firm has had to make do with BRA 1G.

Turtles mate at four o'clock in the afternoon and lay their eggs at six.

So much water floods from the Amazon into the Atlantic that ships out of sight of land can draw up fresh water.

QUEEN Elizabeth I sanctioned a law obliging everybody over the age of seven to wear a flat cap on Sundays and holidays. Only lords, ladies and knights with an income of over 20 marks a year were exempt.

Enough cannabis was brought into the United States in 1973 to roll each inhabitant 20 joints.

Until the 16th century rich bodies were buried inside churches in England and paupers outside. The inscription on a gravestone at Kingsbridge, Devon, reads: "Here I lie at the chancel door, Here I lie because I'm poor, The further in the more you'll pay, Here I lie as warm as they."

MILOSH Obrenovich, formerly a pig dealer, became ruler of Serbia in 1830.

ABORIGINES at Pulykara in the Gibson Desert, Australia, saw their first white man in 1969.

An enthusiastic crowd applauded Councillor Stanley Webb of Market Drayton, Shropshire, when, accompanied by a brass band, he cut the ribbon to open officially his council's new public lavatory. He had drunk champagne all morning so that his inaugural effort would give the urinal the best possible christening, and had asked the band to accompany him with Handel's Water Music. As this was beyond their scope, the band compromised with The March of the Peers.

A SUMO wrestler lunches on 10 lb. of rice, chicken, fish and vegetables, washed down with beer. For supper he tucks away 7 lb. of stew.

Corpses entering Scotland from England must be accompanied by an Out-of-England order.

IN THE 16th-century it was thought perfectly proper to sleep naked, but highly indecent to wear a shift in bed.

A NEW YORK State law controlling massage parlours was so sweeping that, if enforced, it would have closed down the whirl-pool bath at the YMCA, the locker room at the Yankee Stadium, every doctors' surgery, and limited all physical contact to shaking hands.

NATURALLY odourless, nylon sails, ropes and fishnet were impregnated with the scent of rotting hemp and ripe docksides to make them more acceptable to conservative fishermen.

The only way to obtain liquor in certain dry Indian states is with a medical certificate declaring the bearer to be a chronic alcoholic unable to survive without a regular dose.

POTENTIAL suicides in Bloemfontein, South Africa, can apply for help to a day-and-night Life-Line centre. Before you can be saved, however, you must first satisfy the organisers that you are white and have paid your Life-Line subscription.

A HUNGRY walrus will take a pre-lunch snack of fist-sized stones to help digestion.

WHEN muffs reached their most fashionable extremes in the 16th century, spoon handles had to be lengthened.

London's street and parks receive a daily deluge of a million pints of urine and 70 tons of excrement from the capital's dogs.

CREMATION was re-established in Britain in the last century by William Price who, at the age of 84, burned the corpse of his baby son, named Jesus Christ, in whom he hoped to be reincarnated. Price's housekeeper sold tickets for the ceremony which attracted such a crowd that it took 37 policemen to keep order.

Queen Elizabeth I owned 2000 dresses.

SCALED up in size and speed, the common house spider could give a world champion sprinter eight seconds start and still beat him over 100 metres.

ONE-FIFTH of Britain's housewives buy corned beef at least once a week, and altogether their families get through 18 million lb. of it every year. Laid end to end, the cans would stretch the 7000 miles from London to Omaha, Nebraska.

AN EARLY 19th-century gentleman hired an artist to paint day-by-day portraits of his mistress to illustrate her decline and eventual death from consumption.

IF YOU sleep beneath 5 lb. of blankets and breathe the average 16 times a minute, by the time you wake up after an eight-hour sleep your chest will have lifted 16 tons.

THE buttock muscle is the largest in the human body.

TWO male prisoners in San Quentin prison who got married by mail order sued the governor for violating their constitutional rights by refusing to allow them to share a cell.

MERTHYR TYDFIL has the highest density of betting shops in Britain—one for every thousand inhabitants.

A professional sandcastle builder at Weymouth uses sand, seawater and watercolour paints to create tableaux ranging from the Last Supper to the Mad Hatter's Tea Party.

WHEN Rodney Hill bought the original *Morning Cloud* from Edward Heath he renamed it *Morning After* and christened the yacht's tender *Enoch*.

CHILDREN of Anglo Saxons had to be tough to survive. To test their courage they were placed on a sloping roof or the bough of a tree. Laughter meant life; crying brought instant death.

SUNSPOTS fluctuate in an 11-year cycle. So do stock exchange and wheat prices, admissions to mental hospitals, and accidents in Chicago.

Early Wild West first-aiders cauterised rattlesnake bites with burning gunpowder.

SLOTHS spend an average of 10 hours every week awake but motionless; 11 hours feeding; 18 hours climbing; and 129 hours asleep.

THE Great Western Railway Bill of the 1840s made the company liable for a £20 fine for every locomotive or carriage discovered using the tracks on the Lord's Day.

FISH and chip sales in Brighton and Blackpool invariably hit a peak during Labour Party conferences, but slump badly when the Tories are in town.

The coloured population of Cape Town hold an annual Coon Carnival.

THE average human scalp sprouts 120,000 hairs. Natural blondes have as many as 140,000; redheads as few as 90,000.

HALF-A-MILLION locusts—a small fraction of an average swarm—consume as much food in a day as 250 people.

THE Original Great Barrier Pigeongram Service of New Zealand used to run an airmail service between Auckland and the Hen and Chicken Islands.

IBRAHIM, a 17th-century Sultan of Turkey, once had his entire harem of several hundred women tied up in sacks and dropped into the Bosphorus, simply to give himself an excuse to gather a new one.

It is a criminal offence to drive a dirty car in the Soviet Union.

IN Saigon, the comet Kohoutek was blamed for the steeply rising price of rice, the shelling of Bien Hoa airport and the imposition of Value Added Tax.

THE Niagara Falls are turned off at night after the tourists have gone home. A hydro-electric plant upstream needs the water.

Bermondsey, London, had one lavatory for every 25 houses in 1898.

ANY CHANCE OF
A QUICK CANCELLATION?
'E'S BIN SCRUMPIN'
AGAIN

ALSO AVAILABLE IN CORONET BOOKS